BYZANTINE AND VENETIAN CRETE
A HISTORIC NOTE

In 395 AD, the vast Roman Empire was divided into two states: the Eastern Empire, with Constantinople as its capital, and the Western Empire, under Rome. Crete, which formed part of the Prefecture of Illyricum, composed of the Dioceses of Dacia and Macedonia (southern Albania, mainland Greece excepting Thrace, the Ionian Islands, the western Aegean and Crete), became an administrative part of the Eastern Roman Empire, later to be named Byzantium.

The autonomous Church of Crete, however, remained under the jurisdiction of the Pope of Rome until 732-33, when it was annexed to the Church of the Eastern Empire by the iconoclast Emperor Leo III Isaurus, in reprisal for the Pope's support of the iconolaters.

In 827-28 Crete was occupied by the Arabs of Spain, who transferred the capital from Gortyna in Messara to the north coast where they founded a new capital, Khandax, where Heraklion stands today.

The Iberian Arab occupation of Crete was a serious blow to the security of Byzantine shipping in the Aegean and the eastern Mediterranean, as the conquerors, using Crete as a base of operations, raided and pillaged the Aegean islands and the coasts of Asia Minor, regions belonging to the Byzantine Empire.

Although Byzantine military operations for the liberation of Crete began immediately after its occupation, the island was to remain under the Arab yoke for about 134 years, until 961 AD when it was liberated by General Nicephorus Phocas, later to become Emperor.

The loss of Crete was as great a blow to the Arabs and the entire Arab world as it had earlier been to the Byzantines, a fact demonstrated by the upheavals and massacres of Christians in Egypt at the news of the fall of Arab Khandax to the Byzantines.

In the following period, Crete, now part of the Byzantine Empire once more, was raised to the status of a theme, governed by a general. Administrative and religious order was restored, as were the island's intellectual and artistic ties to Constantinople, the capital of the Empire. In the 12th century Crete was at the peak of prosperity, a fact mainly attested by archaeological evidence. In 1204, on the eve of the Fourth Crusade, the island was sold by Alexius Angelus, son of the deposed Emperor Isaac, to Boniface of Montferrat, leader of the Fourth Crusade, in exchange for his father's restoration to the throne of Byzantium. Boniface in turn sold Crete to the Venetians for 1,000 silver marks. The Venetians did not immediately take control of the island, a fact exploited by the Genoese pirate Enrico Pescatore who occupied Crete in 1206, thereby "forcing" Venice to attend to its possession and drive him from the island, after a vicious war, in 1210-11.

During the course of the 13th century the Venetians attempted to consolidate their domination of the island, fighting the local Byzantine nobility, the "Roman lords", and the Cretan people, who resisted with all their might. In 1299 the Venetians were forced to sign a peace treaty with the most eminent Byzantine nobleman, Alexios Kallergis, by the terms of which he and the local nobility wrested substantial privileges from the Venetians. The Cretan rebellions continued throughout the period of the Venetian occupation, albeit at far longer intervals. The long periods of peace and the economic prosperity of the island led to the development of Venetocretan culture, which emerged from the union of Byzantine and Venetian elements.

The cultural and economic flourishing of Crete was interrupted by the Turkish occupation, achieved in 1669 with the surrender to the Turks of the capital, Khandax. The siege of Khandax by the Turks had lasted almost twenty-five years, making it the longest siege in history, and ended with a treaty of surrender according to which the Venetians were allowed to leave the city with their archives and heirlooms. Many Cretans abandoned the city with the Venetians, taking the road to exile.

INFORMATION ON THE SETTLEMENT OF KRITSA, THE CHURCH AND ITS DONORS

The settlement of Kritsa lies 300m. above sea level, south of the town of Agios Nikolaos, the capital of Lassithi Province. Although the date of its foundation is unknown, it certainly existed in 1328, forming part of the family fief of the Venetian nobleman Marco Cornaro.

The registration of the Cornaro estate shows that the main activity of the inhabitants of Kritsa at the time was animal husbandry, followed by agriculture.

The name of the village in the 14th century was Grece (dele Grece) in the Venetian dialect, while its Greek inhabitants at the time called it Kritzea, as the painted dedicatory inscription in the south aisle of the Church of Our Lady shows. In 1633 Venetian sources give the name of the settlement as Crices.

The two dedicatory inscriptions of the church, preserved in the south aisle dedicated to St Anne and the north aisle dedicated to St Antony, bear three names and surnames belonging to its principal donors. In the south aisle of St Anne the donors are Antonios Lameras and Eiginios, known as Sinouletos. In the north aisle of St Antony the donor is George Mazizanis, who is depicted with his wife and daughter on the north wall of the aisle. However apart from these principal, and therefore named, donors, all the inhabitants of the village of Kritzea also contributed to the costs of the church wall paintings, a fact commemorated on the inscription.

In the central aisle, dedicated to the Dormition of the Virgin, there were two inscriptions: one on the scene of Christ with the praying Virgin, and one by the scene of St George, over a possible original secondary entrance; both inscriptions are lost. The first inscription was a prayer, while the second seems to have been dedicatory.

It should be noted that dedicatory inscriptions are connected to the wall painting of churches but not necessarily their construction, which was often undertaken by feudal lords, both Greek and Venetian, for the use of their vassals. The donors who bore the greater financial burden or even the full cost of construction usually had rights of ownership over the church, such as a percentage of its income, the choice of its priest and the right to be buried within it.

The church of Our Lady, which acquired its present form gradually with the addition of the side aisles to the central one, belongs to the architectural type of the three-aisled domed basilica (fig. 1). The main entrance is in the west side of the central aisle, with a secondary entrance in the south wall of the south aisle.

The interior of the church is dimly lit by two pointed gothic windows piercing the west walls of the south and north aisles

FIG. 1: Our Lady at Kritsa. View from the southeast.

respectively, the narrow openings of the three apses and the four windows in the dome.

Of the three aisles, the central one – dedicated to the Dormition of the Virgin– is almost double the width of the others, although all three are the same length.

The semicircular bema (chancel) apses are placed, as usual, at the east ends of the aisles and covered by quarter domes, apart from the central apse which is covered by a recessed roof and is higher and wider than the two side apses (fig. 2).

FIG. 2: Our Lady at Kritsa. View from the east.

The central aisle is covered by a barrel vault whose central part is interrupted by a cylindrical squat dome with a conical roof. The south aisle is also roofed by a barrel vault, while the north aisle has a slightly pointed (gothic) vault, a type found in most churches of the Venetian period. Most of the church is roofed with more modern tiles.

Communication between the central and side aisles is though four semicircular arched openings, whose later widening destroyed part of the wall decoration in all three aisles as well as the painted dedicatory inscription, fragments of which are preserved, as we have mentioned, on the south side of the north party wall, between the scene of St George and the north-west arched passageway (fig. 3). The inscription may have followed the common practice of mentioning the date and the name of the contemporary emperor of Byzantium.

The three different building phases of the church are still discernible today. The transformation of the church into a three-aisled basilica with the addition of the side aisles and the opening and widening of the arched passageways had already been completed by the 14th century, as we will see below.

FIG. 3: Our Lady at Kritsa. Central aisle. North-west arch. Dedicatory inscription.

THE ORIGINAL CHURCH

The central aisle of the church was originally a self-contained single-aisled church with a dome, an architectural type represented locally by the church of Agios Nikolaos (8th/9th c.?) in the town of the same name about 12 km from Kritsa, which contains wall paintings dated to the Iconoclastic Period (decorative designs) and later.

This type, the simplest cross-in-square plan, appeared in Byzantine church architecture in the 8th century, during the Iconoclastic Controversy. Most of the few single-aisled domed churches preserved in Crete are dated to the 11th or 12th century, that is to the Second Byzantine Period (961-1204) of Cretan history.

Although the building of the original single-aisled domed church which now forms the central aisle of the church of Our Lady has been dated to the 13th century, the construction of the dome –unique to Crete and rare elsewhere, with its projecting poros stone ribs (fig. 4), heavy proportions and awkward construction, culminating in a squat shape widening at the base, as well as the recessed apse roof, also an archaic form– point to a far earlier date.

The ribs characteristic of Constantinople church construction construction are found, rarely, in mainland Greece and Cyprus from the 10th to the 11th century, mainly on groin vaults but very rarely on domes. It is therefore highly unlikely that an archaic and rare building style would be preserved into, or rediscovered in, the 13th century. Thus, according to architectural data, the original church of Our Lady must be dated to the end of the Second Byzantine Period, i.e. the late 12th century. We do not know whether that original church contained wall paintings, although it is probable. The oldest preserved wall painting in the central aisle, fragments of which are preserved in the bema and the tympanum of the north and south arches of the dome, has been dated to the mid-13th century. However, the first impression is of 12th-century art, as it includes many of the characteristics of the period.

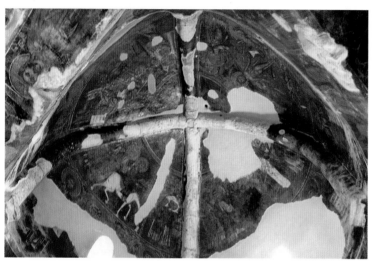

FIG. 4: Our Lady at Kritsa. Central aisle.
The projecting poros stone ribs are visible.

THE ADDITION OF THE SIDE AISLES

Around the late 13th century, the church was repaired after small-scale damage of unknown cause. The side aisles were then added, transforming the church into a three-aisled building. The side aisles communicated with the central aisle through a disused entrance to the original church (probably in the west section of its north wall, under the destroyed dedicatory inscription), a new entrance opened in the east part of the same wall, and two others at the ends of what was now the south party wall. All the passages were arched and

FIG. 5a: Our Lady at Kritsa. South aisle.
"Lintel" of the south-east arched passageway.

originally much narrower, as evidenced by the decorative "lintel" preserved above the north front of the south-east arched passageway. After the completion of the building work, including the construction of the north aisle, the central aisle was redecorated with the exception of its ends, i.e. the bema apse and the east walls, where the first layer of paintings was preserved. After the walls of the side aisles had also been painted, around the mid-14th century, the four arched passageways – their lintels similarly decorated with painted, almost schematic flowers (figs. 5a,b,c) – were widened: the south-east passageway on its eastern side and the three others on their western sides. This placed the north-west and south-west passageways on the same transverse axis, making all four the same width and thereby unifying the interior of what had now become the architectural type of a three-aisled church. During the same phase another arched passageway was opened to connect the bema of the central aisle to that of the north aisle. After the painting of the north aisle, the main entrance to the central aisle also seems to have been widened, another intervention which, like the preceding ones, caused widespread destruction of the wall paintings. The south aisle, which has four blind arches in the corresponding wall and is very narrow, was poorly made at the front of the bema apse and had structural problems which were hastily repaired before the walls were painted. The secondary entrance in the south wall is of much later construction; the window, however, is not, as we can see from the wall paintings of the west wall, adapted to surround the window opening. The window arches in the side aisles are of poros stone, in the gothic style. The main entrance doorway is semicircular, a form dating to the Late Byzantine Period.

The serious structural statics problems of the church, probably due to the successive interventions, rendered it necessary to support the building with six massive buttresses, cautiously dated to the period of the Turkish occupation. Finally, on the west facade, between the pediments of the south and central aisles, there stands a single-arched poros stone bell tower topped by a pediment, of a form that may be dated to the 16th or 17th century.

In the mid-20th century, when the Greek Archaeological Service first undertook restoration work on the church, the wall paintings were found covered by a thick layer of whitewash.

FIG. 5b: Our Lady at Kritsa. South aisle. "Lintel" of the south-west arched passageway.
c. "Lintel" of the north-west arched passageway.

THE SCENES OF THE AISLES

The dedication of the central aisle to the Dormition of the Virgin is not attested by an inscription as is the case with the other two aisles. According to Professor K. Kalokyris, the dedication is due to an 18th-century icon found in the church. Many people had also mistaken the image of St Anne on the quarter dome of the south aisle for a representation of the Virgin, a fact that may have contributed to the more recent dedication.

The aisle of the Dormition of the Virgin is decorated on the vault and the dome with scenes from the Gospel cycle, while the side walls bear depictions of isolated saints. The south aisle, that of St Anne, is decorated on the vault with scenes from the Apocrypha concerning the life of St Anne and St Joachim, the parents of the Virgin, and the latter's life until the eve of Christ's birth. The side walls consist of two zones in the upper of which are depicted bust portraits of saints, with full-length figures of saints in the lower, wider zone.

The north aisle, that of St Antony, is decorated with scenes of the Last Judgement across the whole vault, as evidenced by the fragments remaining on the north side and the west wall. On the vertical surfaces of the walls of the nave are depicted full-length saints, both male and female. Most of these scenes on the north wall have also flaked off or been destroyed.

CENTRAL AISLE: DORMITION
OF THE VIRGIN
FIRST LAYER OF WALL PAINTINGS

THE APSE AND ITS SIDES

On the quarter dome of the bema was the depiction of the Virgin, enthroned according to the type of the Platytera (Wider than the Heavens); only the lower parts of her blue robe are preserved. To her left and right were the two archangels Michael and Gabriel, of whom only traces remain.

The Virgin, symbol of the incarnation of Jesus and bridge between heaven and earth, is depicted on the quarter dome of the bema from the 5th century onwards. The representation emerged from the Church's attempt to defeat the Monophysite heresy, which accepted only the divine nature of Christ, rejecting his human nature.

On the cylinder of the bema are depicted full-length Church Fathers, turned in three-quarter view towards the centre of the arch, wearing the polystavrion (chasuble marked with crosses) and holding open scrolls, in the iconography of the officiating bishops developed from the 12th century on (fig. 6).

To the viewer's left are depicted the bishops St Nicholas and John Chrysostom, while on the right are St Basil the Great and Gregory the Theologian (figs. 7a,b). Between them is the representation of the Melizomenos or Thyomenos (the Sacrificed One) referring to the Holy Communion, showing the Christ Child in a paten with a spear, between two white-clad archangels who are bowing respectfully, holding ceremonial fans. On the sides of the arch of the apse is the now flaked scene of the Annunciation, with the Archangel Gabriel to the viewer's left and the Virgin to his right.

Under the representation of the archangel of the Annunciation is the bust figure of Deacon Stephen, depicted frontally and beardless, wearing an alb, with a thurible in his left hand and a censer in his right. Deacon Romanus is depicted below the representation of the Virgin of the Annunciation, also frontally but full-length and bearded; the lower part of the figure has been destroyed. He, like Stephen, holds thurible and censer (fig. 8).

THE NAVE

On the tympanum of the south arch of the dome, after the detachment of part of the Pentecost scene on the second layer of wall painting, the frontal bust figure of a female saint bearing the martyr's cross was revealed together with a decorative pattern. The head of a saint and traces of an indecipherable scene were also revealed on the tympanum of the north arch.

FIG. 6: Our Lady at Kritsa. Central aisle. Apse.
First layer of wall paintings.

FIG. 7a: Our Lady at Kritsa. Central aisle. Apse.
St Basil (detail of fig. 6).

FIG. 7b: Our Lady at Kritsa. Central aisle. Apse.
St Gregory the Theologian (detail of fig. 6).

FIG. 8: Our Lady at Kritsa. Central aisle. Apse. South side.
Deacon Romanus.

THE STYLE AND DATING
OF THE EARLIER PAINTINGS
OF THE CENTRAL AISLE

The painting of the first layer, which has been dated to about the mid-13th century, is characterised by light-coloured, flat surfaces spread on a light green foundation, the highlights (white brushstrokes) kept to a minimum, the intense linear contours of the features and outlines, and the detailed rendering of curls and ears (a white capital E or F is formed over the ears), which end in the shape of a singular ornament (figs 7a,b, 8). The eyes are large and almond-shaped with a distinct outline, the pupils black, the glance sidelong and lively. The facial expression, with the soft moulding and discreet contrasts, breathes mildness and solemnity, while the high foreheads imbue the figures with spirituality. The heavily accentuated eyebrows, however, meeting above the bridge of the anticlassical nose, give weight to the face, dividing it into two unequal parts and betraying the popular artist, who remains attached to the traditions of Byzantine art at its 11th and 12th-century peak. These traditions were still strongly evident in early 13th-century Crete, to which the figures of the first layer of Kritsa paintings can be dated.

CENTRAL AISLE
SECOND LAYER OF WALL PAINTINGS

The second layer of wall paintings is preserved on the side, or north and south, walls of the bema, the vault of the bema and the rest of the nave, apart from those parts of the tympana where it has been destroyed, as mentioned above, revealing wall paintings of the first layer.

THE HIERARCHS OF THE SIDE WALLS OF THE BEMA

On the north side wall of the bema are depicted Titus the Apostle, founder and first bishop of the Church of Crete, and the Apostle Andrew. Their bodies were destroyed by the opening of the arched passageway connecting the bemata of the central and north aisles (fig. 9). On the south wall are depicted St Eleutherios – in a poor state of preservation – and St Polycarp, bishop of Smyrna and disciple of St John the Evangelist.

On the north side of the soffit (inner face) of the triumphal arch separating the bema from the nave are depicted, from top to bottom, the Prophet Solomon, full-length and frontal, wearing a crown and royal robes and holding an open scroll, and on the next pier (vertical part of the arch), St Panteleimon and St Kirykos, similarly depicted. On the south side of the

Fig. 9: Our Lady at Kritsa. Central aisle. Bema. North wall.
Ss Titus and Andrew.

soffit are depicted, again from top to bottom, the Prophet David in royal robes and diadem with pendants, in the same iconographical type as Solomon; St Ermolaos; and St Julitta, mother of St Kirykos, whose depiction is connected to that of her son, directly opposite.

THE ASCENSION

After the Resurrection, Christ appeared to two of his disciples and dined with them at Emmaus without their recognising him. At the supper Christ blessed the bread and broke it between them, as he had done at the Last Supper. Then the disciples were enlightened and recognised him, but he disappeared and they returned at once to Jerusalem, where they met the others and told them what had happened. Before they could finish their tale, Christ suddenly reappeared before them, greeting them with the words "*Peace be unto you*". His sudden appearance terrified the disciples, who took him for a vision. Christ was aware of their fear and doubt and urged them to examine and touch the wounds from the nails, and asked them for food so they could see he was no vision. At this meeting he revealed to them that they would go out and preach his teaching throughout the world, beginning in Jerusalem. He promised them that God would help them achieve their difficult task by imbuing them with the Holy Spirit, and told them not to leave Jerusalem until that should occur. Then he led them out towards Mount Olive, where he blessed them and was carried up to heaven. The disciples were frightened again on seeing this, but were reassured by two angels who appeared and explained that their teacher was taken up into Heaven to sit on the right hand of his Father until his Second Coming to earth.

The representation of the Ascension is always depicted on the vault of the bema (fig. 10). At its centre is Christ enthroned in a circular glory, raised to heaven by four angels. To the left and right of the Ascending Christ are depicted the two choirs of Apostles with the Virgin, who watch him shaken and praying, while he blesses them. Two angels, one in each choir, reassure them explaining the Ascension (fig. 11). In the north choir, where the Virgin is also depicted, Paul can be seen holding his 14 epistles in a red letter-case (fig. 12).

THE SCENES OF THE DOME

The dome, according to the interpretation of the parts of the church by Photios, Patriarch of Constantinople, is the symbol of heaven where Christ resides, while its lower parts, the vertical surfaces of the side walls and the corresponding section of the west wall under the tympanum of the pediment, symbolise earth, where the saints were born and suffered martyrdom and where the faithful live. Thus on the upper parts of the nave is depicted the Gospel cycle, i.e. the life of

Fig. 10: Our Lady at Kritsa. Central aisle. Bema vault. Ascension (detail).

FIG. 11: Our Lady at Kritsa. Central aisle. Bema vault. North section.
Choir of Apostles and the Virgin (detail).

FIG. 12: Our Lady at Kritsa. Central aisle. Bema vault. South section. Choir of Apostles (detail).

Christ on earth, while on the lower parts are the saints and martyrs, the soldiers of the faith. The iconography of the dome was predetermined, as were the iconographic cycles of every part of the church. In the 13th century the iconographic scheme of the dome was composed of the representation of Christ Pantokrator (Ruler over All) at the crown, angels and prophets on the tympanum (fig. 13a) and the four Evangelists in the pendentives (triangles at the intersection of dome and arches).

FIG. 13a: Our Lady at Kritsa. Central aisle. Dome.
Prophet Isaiah and indistinct figure (detail).

The common points between this established decoration and the decoration of Kritsa are the four Evangelists in the pendentives and the angels between the Evangelists and the Prophets in the second zone of the tympanum (fig. 13b). The differences lie in the scenes from the Gospels and the four cherubim at the crown of the dome. Gospel scenes on the tympanum of the dome are found in the Church of Peter and

FIG. 13b: Our Lady at Kritsa. Central aisle. Dome. Luke the Evangelist.

Paul at Novi Pazar in the former Yugoslavia, dated to the 10th century. There must have been intervening monuments between Novi Pazar and Kritsa, some of them in Crete itself, forming the model for the iconography of the church of Our Lady. Of course a determining part in the decoration of the dome with Gospel scenes was played by its projecting ribs, which prevented the representation of Christ Pantokrator at the crown. The established depiction therefore had to be replaced by other Christological scenes which would stress the dual nature of Christ, both human and divine, in conjunction with the major Prophets, the cherubim, the angels and the Evangelists. However, the decoration of the central aisle is generally characterised by an archaic style blended with innovative elements, whereas the decoration of the dome is unique in Greece and a rarity elsewhere.

The dome of Kritsa is divided into four triangular interstices by two crossing projecting ribs, containing scenes from the Christological cycle that stress his dual nature, human and divine. In the four triangular interstices, which are subdivided into three horizontal zones, are depicted Cherubim in the upper zone; the Presentation in the Temple, the Baptism, the Entry into Jerusalem and the Raising of Lazarus in the middle zone; and full-length figures of the Prophets in the third and last zone. The pendentives contain the four Evangelists and between them the frontal bust figures of the four archangels Michael, Gabriel, Raphael and Uriel.

Now let us turn to the scenes depicting religious episodes from the life of Christ, the singular Bible of illiterate Christians.

THE PRESENTATION IN THE TEMPLE

According to the Law of Moses, firstborn boys –who were considered holy– had to be presented to the Temple of Jerusalem forty days after their birth. The presentation, if the parents were poor, was accompanied by an offering of a pair of turtledoves or two young pigeons. Joseph and Mary took Jesus to the Temple, where they offered two young white pigeons. There they met an aged, just man of Jerusalem named Simeon, to whom the Holy Ghost had revealed that he should not see death before he had seen the Son of God. Simeon, taking Jesus in his arms, realised that this was the Son of God and cried out, *"Lord, now lettest thou thy servant depart in peace"*. Simeon was not the only one to recognise the divine nature of Christ; so did the Prophetess Anna, granddaughter of Patriarch Jacob, who had served in the Temple for many years without ever leaving it. According to tradition, she said *"This small babe hath made fast heaven and earth"*.

The scene of the Presentation in the Temple depicts Jesus' presentation by Joseph and Mary and the meeting with Simeon and Anna (fig. 14). The background is composed of two tall tower-like buildings with two-sided tiled roofs, on each side of a lower columned building. On the viewer's left is Joseph with two pigeons in his hands, the customary offering, and before him is Mary with outstretched arms, showing that Simeon has just taken Jesus in his own. Jesus, like any baby in the same situation, is turning towards his mother, a depiction implying the human nature of Christ and also revealing the influence of Paleologue iconography, which is concerned with humanity and reality. Simeon holds the white-clad Jesus in his arms, bending his knees, perhaps due to his advanced age, his emotion, or even the divine "weight" of Jesus. Behind Simeon is depicted the Prophetess Anna, with her right hand raised to heaven praising God, while in her left she holds an open scroll bearing the words: *This small babe hath made fast heaven and earth.*

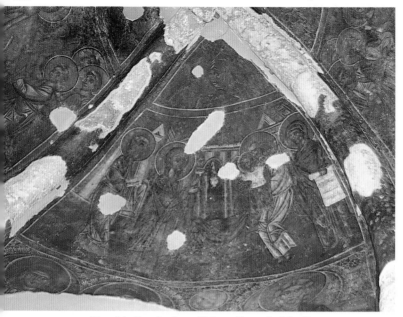

FIG. 14: Our Lady at Kritsa. Central aisle. Dome.
The Presentation in the Temple.

THE BAPTISM

After the death of King Herod, an angel of the Lord told
Joseph to return to Judaea. But Herod's son Archelaus now
reigned there, and Joseph preferred to settle in Nazareth, a
small village in Galilee. At the same time, John the Baptist, the
son of Elizabeth, an enlightened ascetic who lived in the desert
clad in a camel hide and eating tender shoots (*akrides*,
formerly mistakenly translated as locusts) and wild honey,
began to preach the word of God to prepare the coming of
Christ. This is why he is called Prodromos (the Forerunner).
When John began preaching many people went to listen to
him and be baptized in the River Jordan. Jesus also went to
the Jordan to be baptized, but John recognised him and
refused, calling himself unworthy. Jesus, however, reminded
him of the prophecies and John obeyed. While Jesus was in the
river, the heavens opened and the Holy Ghost in the form of a
dove alighted on his head, while the voice of God was heard
from heaven, saying *"This is my beloved Son, in whom I am
well pleased"*.

At the centre of the scene Christ is depicted, naked, with his hands extended out from his body forming an imaginary rhombus, in the River Jordan. The river is lake-shaped with an angled bank to the viewer's left, next to which stands John the Baptist (fig. 15). The latter figure is lost except for the saint's feet and the hem of his sheepskin, as well as his palms, the left raised in prayer and the right on Christ's head. On the right bank are three angels, turned towards Christ and the Baptists, extending their hands, covered by the himation (cloak), in prayer. The Holy Ghost in the form of a dove has been destroyed. In the river can be seen personifications of Jordan and the Sea, fish and a sailing ship, iconographical elements reminiscent of survivals of Hellenistic art. The depiction of Christ is intensely masonic, his body twisting to the right from the waist down in order to hide the sex, and with a distinctive swollen abdomen.

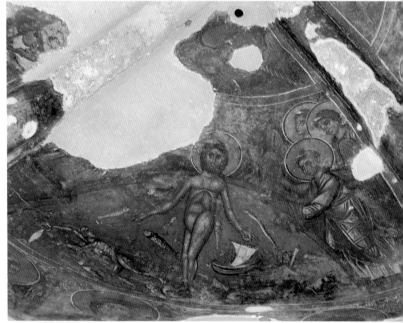

FIG. 15: Our Lady at Kritsa. Central aisle. Dome.
The Baptism.

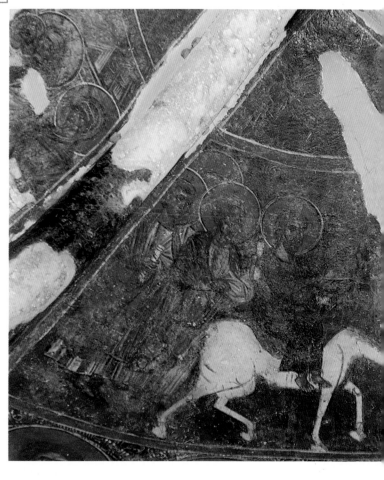

THE ENTRY INTO JERUSALEM

Christ, accompanied by his disciples, visited many cities in Israel, teaching and healing many who believed in him. From Jericho, the last city, he headed to Jerusalem. Arriving in Bethphage just outside Jerusalem, he sent two disciples to the nearby village to bring him an ass's colt whereon never man had sat, which they would find tied at the entrance of the village. If any man should prevent them, they should say that the Lord had need of it and would send it back straight away. All this was done, so that the prophecies of Isaiah and Zechariah concerning his entry into Jerusalem would be fulfilled. The disciples spread their garments on the foal and Christ

F<small>IG</small>. 16: Our Lady at Kritsa. Central aisle. Dome. The Entry into Jerusalem.

rode it. Meanwhile, it was generally known that Christ had raised Lazarus four days after his funeral, and so a multitude of people collected at his arrival, spreading their garments and palms where he would pass, while those that went before cried "*Hosanna, blessed is he that cometh in the name of the Lord*". Thus Christ passed through the excited crowd and came to the Temple of Jerusalem, five days before Passover. Among the crowd were some Pharisees who, seeing the people's love for Christ, considered that he should be arrested as soon as possible.

The scene of the Entry into Jerusalem depicts Christ's welcome before the Gate of Jerusalem (fig. 16). In the background to the right can be seen buildings with tiled roofs, the city walls and the gate, towards which Christ is heading on the white colt. Behind him are three disciples –Peter and John among them– and before him are the fragmentary remains of a tree, by whose trunk is a white-clad child spreading palms in the road. At the gate in the walls a group of Jews is waiting to receive him. The figure of Christ is in the centre of the scene in large scale. The two groups, of disciples to the left and Jews to the right, are arranged in a triangle, in an attempt to render depth. The main colours of the scene are the white of the colt; the red of the himatia (cloaks) of two disciples and a Jew, the roofs and the colt's saddle-cloth; the light grey of the tunics of both groups; and the brick-red of the earth. Christ is wearing a brown tunic and deep green himation.

THE RAISING OF LAZARUS

Christ was at the River Jordan when he learned that Lazarus, the brother of Mary and Martha from Bethany, was gravely ill. Although he loved Lazarus deeply, Christ was not worried at the news of his health, saying that this sickness was for the glory of God and his Son. After a few days Christ went to Bethany, where he found that Lazarus had died four days earlier. Christ, however, was not disturbed even then, but asked to be taken to the grave, a cave closed by a great stone. He asked them to take away the stone and called Lazarus forth, and all present saw Lazarus come forth from the grave. Christ asked a slave to remove the winding-sheet and let Lazarus walk home.

The scene depicts Christ on the left, at the head of a small group of disciples with Peter at the front. Kneeling in the centre and worshipping Christ are Lazarus' sisters Mary and Martha, the latter turning her head towards her brother's grave. To the right is the risen Lazarus in his winding-sheet, which is being unwrapped by a Jew, and behind him a group of Jews (fig. 17). The scene has suffered severe damage. The figure of the slave covering his nose with his himation because of the stink of Lazarus is partly destroyed.

FIG. 17: Our Lady at Kritsa. Central aisle. Dome.
The Raising of Lazarus.

THE SCENES OF THE VAULT

On the south section of the vault the following scenes are preserved, from east to west: above, the Nativity and the Descent into Hell; below, the Massacre of the Infants and Paradise. On the corresponding northern section of the vault, from west to east, are the following scenes: Herod's Feast, the Holy of Holies and the Last Supper. The largely destroyed scene was the Betrayal.

THE NATIVITY

When the Roman decree of a tax census was issued, Joseph and his family, Mary and his two sons, had to travel to Bethlehem to be taxed. According to the Apocryphal Gospel of James, shortly before they arrived in Bethlehem Mary felt the pangs of childbirth. Despite Joseph's protests, she and his sons took refuge in a cave in the wilderness, while he went in search of a midwife in Bethlehem. According to St Luke, Christ was born in the town of Bethlehem, in a stable where Joseph found shelter because the inns were full of travellers. The first to learn of the joyful event were shepherds keeping watch over their flock by night.

The scene is dominated by the figure of the Virgin, who is roughly three times the size of the other figures (fig. 18). She is depicted sitting relaxed, with a calm face, a sign of her painless birth. Behind her in a stone manger is the infant Jesus in swaddling-clothes. In the corner to the viewer's left, Joseph is sitting sunk in thought, his head resting on his hand. Next to him the midwife Salome bathes the child in a marble basin on a tall pedestal like a font. Above Joseph the Wise Men bring

FIG. 18: Our Lady at Kritsa. Central aisle. Nave. Vault.
The Nativity.

their gifts, while angels sing praises on the roof of the cave and the shepherds with their animals approach its entrance. The iconography of the scene is found in wall paintings, icons and manuscripts from the 8th century onwards.

THE MASSACRE OF THE INNOCENTS

Before the birth of Christ, three wise men, magi and astronomers from the East, saw a bright star in the east announcing the birth of the King of the Jews. Guided by the star, the wise men journeyed to Judaea to worship him. When they arrived in Jerusalem the star vanished, so they asked where the new king had been born. When King Herod heard that a new king was born, he was angry and demanded of the Chief Priests and Scribes what the prophecies said. They replied that the Prophet Micah had written that the greatest ruler of the world would be born in Bethlehem. Herod cunningly called the wise men secretly to him and asked them how long ago they had seen the star, so he could calculate Jesus' age. He then sent them to Bethlehem and asked them to bring him word when they had found the child, so that he could go and worship him also. The wise men, led by the star which had reappeared as soon as they left Jerusalem, found Jesus, worshipped him and offered him gold, frankincense and myrrh. But an angel of the Lord warned them not to inform Herod but to depart into their country by another way. At the same time, another angel told Joseph to flee secretly into Egypt with Mary and Jesus.

When Herod realised that he was waiting for the wise men in vain, he ordered his soldiers to slay all the children in Bethlehem and its environs under two years of age. Then there was great weeping and lamentation, fulfilling the prophecy of Jeremiah that even Rachel, the dead wife of Patriarch Jacob, would weep inconsolably for the children of her descendants.

The scene of the Massacre of the Innocents, its cruelty tempered by the popular artist, depicts the brutal slaying of the infants by Herod's soldiers, the lamentation of Rachel and the pursuit of Elizabeth and her son John the Baptist –who was about Christ's age– by the soldiers, as well as the mountain which opened to hide them from their persecutors (fig. 19).

On the viewer's left is Herod seated on his throne with a guard behind him. The figure of Herod is the largest in this scene, followed by that of his armoured guard. In front of the king on two levels are depicted his soldiers in helmets and chain mail, bearing lances on which are skewered the slaughtered babies and infants. The west part of the scene depicts Elizabeth with John the Baptist inside the mountain that opened to conceal them from Herod's soldiers, and next to it the soldier who had been chasing them. Under the mountain are three severed heads, and the vertical axis ends in

FIG. 19: Our Lady at Kritsa. Central aisle. Nave. Vault.
The Massacre of the Innocents.

the figure of Rachel the Just, the foremother of Jesus, weeping for the children of Israel. In her apron are the severed heads of three children.

THE DESCENT INTO HELL (ANASTASIS)

According to the Apocryphal Gospel of Bartholomew, the latter remained on Golgotha until nightfall, when he saw that Christ had vanished from the cross and heard wailing and gnashing of teeth. At the first meeting of Christ and his disciples after the Resurrection, Bartholomew asked him where he went from the cross. Christ explained that he went down into Hell to bring life and resurrection to the dead imprisoned in the darkness. According to the Apocryphal Gospel of Nicodemus, Adam, the father of the whole race of men, together with all the patriarchs and prophets of Israel, saw the purple light of the sun shining in the depths of Hell and immediately remembered the Creator, who had promised them everlasting light. The Prophet Isaiah reminded them of his prophecy of the light "of the Father and of the Son", which was to rise upon the dead, while Simeon reminded them of his enlightenment by the Holy Ghost at Christ's Presentation in the Temple, which made him speak of the salvation of all people by the holy child. Immediately afterwards St John the Baptist appeared, confirming Christ's descent into Hell, which was announced by a voice as of thunder commanding the rulers of Hell to remove the Gates and let the King of Glory pass through. And Christ appeared lighting the darkness, trampling the gates and chains of Hell underfoot and freeing Adam.

The scene of the Descent into Hell is extensively damaged and destroyed. Its iconography is brief and vividly archaic in character.

The prophet-kings David and Solomon, who prophesied the coming of Christ, are represented from the waist up, rising from marble tombs whose interior is lit by the scarlet glory of Christ (fig. 20). David and Solomon wear royal diadems and garments dyed a characteristic red. Above are John the Baptist and probably the Prophet Isaiah. Both figures have flaked,

34

FIG. 20: Our Lady at Kritsa. Central aisle. Nave. Vault. The Descent into Hell (detail).

but we can see their hands in the attitude of prayer, their dark tunics and their deep brown himatia. In the centre, Christ is depicted in large scale, in an orange-red glory, rushing in, with the upper part of his body turning to his left, with his right hand drawing Adam up from a marble tomb –his halo and figure are dimly visible– while turning right from the waist down; he treads on the broken gates of Hell on tiptoe. Despite the destruction and flaking of the scene, Christ's obvious rushing movement as he draws the kneeling Adam up from the dark prison of Hell, combined with the intense scarlet of the glory and the tombs of the prophet kings, allow the scene to retain its dramatic character. Christ is wearing a deep grey tunic and a himation of deep golden orange draped above his right knee in consecutive triangles, a depiction underlining the rush of his descent.

PARADISE

The scene is dominated by the frontal praying figure of the Virgin, seated on a high throne with a red footstool decorated with pearls (fig. 21). She is wearing a dark tunic and a deep brown maphorion (robe). To her right is depicted the Good Thief Gesdas, to whom Christ had promised a place in Paradise, holding a cross in his right hand and praying with his left, outside the Gate of Paradise, which is guarded by a flaming sword. The Thief is wearing only the white loincloth of his crucifixion. To the left of the Virgin, in a line with her but on a lower level, the forefathers Isaac, Abraham and Jacob, seated on thrones with red footstools, bear in a triple mandorla the souls of the righteous in the form of white-clad boys viewed in bust. The forefathers, wearing dark green tunics and brown himatia, are portrayed in a frontal pose which is moderated by the depiction of the lower legs, the direction of the gaze, the imperceptible turn of Abraham's head to his left and Isaac's to his right. The facial expressions indicate the solemnity of the ceremony of the Last Judgement, while the tall fruit-bearing trees and white background denote the idyllic and peaceful atmosphere of Paradise.

FIG. 21: Our Lady at Kritsa. Central aisle. Nave. Vault. Paradise.

HEROD'S FEAST

Herod Antipas, tetrarch of Galilee, imprisoned John the Baptist for accusing him of marrying his brother Philip's wife, Herodias. However Herod did not immediately dare kill John because the people loved him. But he was to do so soon. On his birthday Herod held a feast for his friends which was attended by Herodias and her daughter Salome. Salome danced so beautifully for Herod that he promised to give her anything she wanted. At her mother's urging, she asked for the head of John the Baptist.

The iconography of the scene is developed behind and to the right of the horizontal axis of the table that dominates the

FIG. 22: Our Lady at Kritsa. Central aisle. Nave. Vault. Herod's Feast (detail).

scene, stressed by the white tablecloth and the red drapery bridging the gaps between the tower-like buildings in the background (fig. 22). To the viewer's right the main axis is vertical, with the tall, slender figure of Salome bearing on her head a platter with the Baptist's head and continuing with the bowed figure of the saint and the executioner seen standing ready behind him. On the table are ornate vessels of Venetian glass, silverware, bread and small white radishes.

THE HOLY OF HOLIES (PRESENTATION OF THE VIRGIN)

When Mary was three years old, Joachim and Anne decided it was time to fulfill their promise to God and take their daughter to the Temple. Being afraid that, due to her age, she might react to her presentation, they organised a procession of undefiled daughters of the Hebrews bearing lit tapers to impress her. Mary not only did not try to turn back to her parents, but remained happily in the temple, where she received food from an angel.

The scene entitled the Holy of Holies depicts the arrival at and entry into the Temple of the procession of virgins, Joachim and Anne, led by Mary, and the latter's welcome by the archpriest Zacharias (fig. 23). On the viewer's left are the daughters of the Hebrews, led by the maiden behind St Anne. This maiden is wearing different garments to the others, a white granatza (long coat with loose sleeves) with purple and

FIG. 23: Our Lady at Kritsa. Central aisle. Nave. Vault.
The Holy of Holies (Presentation of the Virgin in the Temple).

a red cloak clasped at the throat, Byzantine dress adopted by Cretan ladies up to the 15th century. A characteristic example is the identically dressed figure of the wife of the donor and owner Mazizanis, in the dedicatory scene in the aisle of St Antony.

Behind Zacharias we can see the scene of the angel feeding the Virgin during her stay in the Temple. The figures are depicted very tall in the west part of the painting, diminishing until Zacharias and attaining their greatest size in the scene of the angel. The artist used this technique to stress the essential subject of the scene, the divine protection surrounding Mary.

THE LAST SUPPER

While the Scribes and Pharisees had decided to organise Christ's arrest after the approaching feast of the Passover, his disciples began to seek a room for the Passover meal. Their teacher sent two of them into Jerusalem, telling them to follow a man bearing a pitcher of water to a house and ask the owner of the house where the guestchamber was, where Christ was to eat the Passover with his disciples. Indeed, the owner showed them an upper room where they prepared the meal.

During the meal Christ revealed to his disciples that one of them would betray him; they were all shaken and began to ask him one by one whether it was they, each seemingly afraid that he was destined for this part by the will of God. Christ told them only that the betrayer dipped his hand with him in the dish. Then Judas said, "*Master, is it I?*", and Christ replied "*Thou hast said it*". Immediately afterwards he blessed the bread and divided it among the disciples, saying "*Take, eat; this is my body*". Doing the same with the wine, he said "*Drink ye all of it; for this is my blood*".

The scene depicts the disturbance caused by Christ's announcement of the betrayal (fig. 24). Most of the disciples have risen from the table, wondering and asking Christ if they are the betrayers, while John, the beloved disciple, has approached him to ask the same thing. The only exception is Judas, who continues to eat, calmly reaching out to the food – the only disciple depicted in profile in every single Byzantine

FIG. 24: Our Lady at Kritsa. Central aisle. Nave. Vault.
The Last Supper.

representation of this moment of the Last Supper. The drama
and disturbance the artist wishes to convey in this scene is
achieved though the facial expressions and gestures of the
disciples.

In the background are three tall, narrow, tower-like
buildings placed at the edges and the centre of the painting. A
red canopy defines the upper limit, linking the three buildings.
The overall composition is horizontal, with Christ on a larger
scale at the left of the scene, at the head of the table, with John
next to him, Peter opposite, Judas in the centre with one hand
reaching out to the fish, and the other disciples between and
behind them. Using superposition instead of his usual basic
perspective, the artist manages to stress the main figures and
the disturbed atmosphere of the scene, despite its undeniable
flatness. The white tablecloth, similar to that in the scene of
Herod's Feast, bears similar tableware and small white
radishes.

THE BETRAYAL

After the Last Supper, Jesus and his disciples went to the Garden of Gethsemane, where he left them for a while in order to pray alone. As he prayed, he bowed under the weight of his coming Passion three times, asking his Father to take away the bitter cup of the Crucifixion from him. After he had returned to his disciples, who had fallen asleep, Judas arrived with the soldiers sent by the Archpriests and Pharisees to arrest him. As agreed beforehand, Judas greeted and kissed Jesus and the soldiers arrested him. Peter, enraged, drew his knife and cut off the ear of Malchus, a servant of the High Priest who had followed the soldiers. Jesus rebuked Peter, saying *"They that take the sword shall perish with the sword"*, and healed Malchus' ear.

The episode of Peter and Malchus is the only one in the scene of the Betrayal preserved intact (fig 25). Next to them can be distinguished the headless figures of Jesus, stretching out his right hand to Peter in rebuke, and Judas, opposite Jesus, as well as the soldiers in armour of overlapping scales standing behind Peter. Peter is kneeling, holding Malchus steady with his left hand and the knife in his right. However, Christ's intervention is forcing him to turn his head towards his teacher, an expression of puzzlement and perplexity evident in his wide eyes and the brown shadow underlining them, and the elongation of his face. The garments of Christ and Judas are deep in colour but flaked, but Judas' russet tunic is still visible. Peter is wearing a deep rose tunic and dark green himation, while Malchus is in a shift, probably the short tunic worn by slaves allowing them to do their manual work more easily. Peter is depicted on a scale almost three times that of Malchus.

THE CRUCIFIXION

Traces of the scene are preserved above the central entrance which was widened, probably after the construction and decoration of the north aisle (figs. 26a,b). The widespread damage to the depiction, especially around the doorway, must be due to this intervention. The central part of the scene, depicting Christ, the Virgin and John, has been destroyed. On the right, at the edge of the scene, we can make out the Bad Thief Dimas (Doumachus according to the Apocryphal Gospels). On the viewer's left, in the south part of the tympanum, is the Good thief Thesdas or Gesdas (Titus in the Apocrypha), with a halo; on the viewer's right is the figure of the centurion Longinus, rendered much larger than the Thief, and three Roman soldiers in profile. This difference in size underlines the importance of Longinus, who recognised Christ's divine nature.

FIG. 25: Our Lady at Kritsa. Central aisle. Nave. Vault. The Betrayal (detail).

THE PLACE OF TORMENTS

In the zone between the Crucifixion and the lintel of the central entrance to the church are depicted the damned, men to the viewer's left and women to the right (figs 26a,b). All are depicted full-length and naked with individual characteristics, with their hands tied behind their backs against a red background symbolising the outer fire. The –presumably repeated ly committed– sins of the damned are stated not only by the inscriptions accompanying the figures, but also by the depiction of the proof or instrument of their sinful deed. In the depiction of the sheep-stealer, for instance, we see a sheep on his shoulders, in that of the man who stole his neighbour's

FIG. 26: Our Lady at Kritsa. Central aisle. West wall. Tympanum. The Crucifixion. a. The Good Thief. b. Centurion, soldiers and Bad Thief.

Fig. 26a: Our Lady at Kritsa. Central aisle. West wall. Tympanum.
Punishments of female sinners.

land while ploughing we see a plough, in that of the prostitute
a serpent threatening her genitals, etc. We are thus informed

Fig. 26b: Our Lady at Kritsa. Central aisle. West wall. Tympanum.
Punishments of male sinners.

of the forms of criminal and moral transgression that weighed on the small society of the village.

THE SCENES OF THE SIDE WALLS OF THE NAVE

On the west side of the south-east pier is the scene of the Deesis (Prayer or Supplication) with the Virgin and Christ but without John the Baptist, who usually forms the third figure of the Deesis, which is therefore also called the Trimorphon (fig. 27). Christ is depicted frontally, on a low platform with his right leg forward and bent. In his left hand he holds the closed book of the Gospels decorated with precious stones, while his right is raised in blessing. The Virgin is depicted to his right, her body turned to the centre of the scene while her face is turned toward the viewer. In the lower zone, between Christ and the Virgin, there can be seen traces of a dedicatory inscription ("Deesis of the servant of God"). The scene is executed in a different style to that of the corresponding depictions of the central aisle. It was painted not only after the addition of the side aisles and the opening of the aisle communication passages, but also after the widening of the latter, because the size and importance of the scene demand a certain distance from the viewer. In addition, Christ's halo, decorated with crosses, is completely different to those in the Christological scenes, while the rendering of his face and the folds of his garments with metallic glints are unrelated to those of the full-length frontal saints of the aisle. However, the artist of this scene must have respected the colour scheme of the adjacent depictions of the central aisle.

On the soffit of the west arch of the dome are depicted Ss Mercurius and Nicetas, with St Sergius, Roman primicerius (senior officer) of the Schola Gentilium unit of the Imperial Bodyguard on the north pier, and his close friend and colleague St Bacchus on the south (fig. 28). On the west face of the north-west pier is depicted St Francis and on the corresponding face of the south-west pier is the Apostle Peter. The depictions on the tympana of the arches have been destroyed.

On the long side walls of the nave are preserved the following depictions: on the south wall, St Anne with the infant Mary and St Andrew (fig. 29); on the north wall, St George on his horse (fig. 30); on the west wall, the Guardian Angel of the church to the right of the entrance, and the Elevation of the Cross with Constantine the Great and his mother Helen to the left.

The depiction of St Anne and the infant Virgin on the south wall is an interesting one, being rendered according to the model of the Virgin Hodegetria, or Indicator of the Way (also

Fig. 27: Our Lady at Kritsa. Central aisle. West face of south-east pillar. Deesis.

FIG. 28: Our Lady at Kritsa. Central aisle. South soffit of west dome arch. St Bacchus.

FIG. 29: Our Lady at Kritsa. Central aisle. South wall. St Anne and Virgin. St Andrew.

Dexiokratousa – Holding on Her Right Arm); St Anne holds Mary on her right arm, the latter dressed as she is when depicted as an adult. The halos in relief are due to Western influences.

Even more interesting is the representation of the Catholic St Francis, depicted as a tall, thin and tonsured figure, holding the book of the Gospels decorated with precious stones in his left hand and raising his right in supplication (fig. 31). His left side as we look at him is shown naked to reveal the stigmata,

FIG. 30: Our Lady at Kritsa. Central aisle. Nave. North wall.
St George.

while the characteristic tonsure of Franciscan monks is
stressed by the unnaturally exaggerated bulging temples under
the ring of hair. The saint is wearing the deep brown habit of
his order, tied at the waist with a rope, and sandals with two
horizontal straps, exactly the same as those of the figure of St
Andrew on the south wall.

The inclusion of St Francis in the iconographic programme
of Orthodox Cretan churches, though unusual, is an
indication – taken together with the western-style armour of
the soldiers and the Venetian glassware depicted in the
church– of Venetian influences on Cretans in the late 13th
century. The choice of St Francis – God's Pauper– could also

be interpreted as a rebuke to the cruel and merciless Venetian landowners who oppressed the Cretans, while the gleaming armour and beautiful luxury vessels are reminiscent of the opulence of Byzantine society in Crete.

FIG. 31: Our Lady at Kritsa. Central aisle. West face of north-west pillar. St Francis. Right, details of his bulging temples and side with stigmata.

THE STYLE AND DATING OF THE SECOND LAYER OF WALL PAINTINGS OF THE CENTRAL AISLE

The artist of the second layer of wall paintings of the central aisle is caught between the old art and the new, hesitant, as one would expect of a good popular artist in a transitional period. His attention is centred on the faces and their expressions, on which he exhausts his artistic ability. Even in the scenes on the dome, which are further from the viewer (remember that we view this painting at a distance), the faces are rendered more carefully than the folds of the garments, which the artist often paints stiff and unyielding, disregarding the moulding and movements of the body to such an extent that the result is reminiscent of a woodcut. The most painstakingly rendered and beautiful faces, on the other hand, (in the Ascension, Herod's Feast, Paradise), despite their weaknesses, reserved expressions and stylised hair, are rendered with discreet moulding and contrasts, expressing virtue and melancholy. The artist's drawing of the mouth and eyebrows, the gestures and countermovement of the forms, also allows him to evoke the atmosphere of the scenes: the agitation of the guests at Herod's feast at the beheading of John the Baptist, that of the Apostles at the Ascension (Paul is treading on Matthew's right foot with his own), the serene expression of the Angels and the Virgin, the peaceful atmosphere of Paradise.

The artist's iconographic models are archaic, a characteristic that becomes more apparent in the iconographical compositions and their placement in areas unusual for the time, as with the painting of the dome – where however it must be stressed once more that the existing projecting ribs limited the artist's options. The six-winged cherubim in place of Christ Pantokrator reminds us of the ancient belief placing them first among the heavenly host, next to the Heavenly Father. This theme had been abandoned in the 11th century and revived in the decoration of the dome in the 12th. Christological scenes on the dome underlining Christ's human and divine nature (as do the four scenes on the dome at Kritsa) are particularly rare and found on far earlier 10th century monuments.

The faces are rendered in a mixed style, using the line to trace the outlines and features, and chiaroscuro to shade in the flesh and its moulding. Female and youthful beardless male faces, however, are depicted flatter than those of mature and aged figures. The luminosity of the light ochre flesh is enhanced by the white highlights down the ridge of the nose, over the eyebrows, under the eyes and along the top of the brow.

The linearity in the tracing of the face is very obvious in the secondary figures, particularly those depicted in profile such as the soldiers in the scenes of the Crucifixion and the Massacre of the Innocents; however, they do not lack expression, a result achieved by the varying directions of the curves forming the features. The hairstyles are stylised and carefully rendered, with discreet mannerist survivals (Matthew in the Ascension).

The space in which the scenes are depicted is completely vague. The viewer has the impression that events are taking place in an open square, for instance, as the background is composed of walls and tall, narrow buildings with red tiled roofs. The perspective is rudimentary and rendered by the triangular arrangement of groups (Entry into Jerusalem, Raising of Lazarus), the ranking of figures on different levels (Massacre of the Innocents), and their superimposition on the architectural elements. The importance of the figures is stressed by the scale on which they are depicted. The dominant figure in the Nativity, for instance, is that of the Virgin. Although both Joseph and Salome are in the foreground, they are about a quarter of Mary's size. The natural environment is also idealised. The trees, the plants, their shapes and fruit are not of this world (Pl. 1, 2).

PL. 1: Our Lady at Kritsa. Central aisle.
Various ways of depicting faces, according to importance, age and sex.

PL. 2: Our Lady at Kritsa. Central aisle.
Depiction of architectural depth, nature and garment folds.

SOUTH AISLE
OF ST ANNE BEMA APSE

On the quarter dome of the apse is a frontal bust portrait of St Anne, and on the front of its arch is Christ-Emmanuel in a medallion (fig. 32). On the cylinder of the bema are depicted the officiating bishops Peter of Alexandria, Gregory, Athanasius and Eleutherius, full-length with their heads slightly bowed as a sign of respect and turned in three-quarter view towards the centre; they are clad in episcopal vestments – sticharia (albs) with jewel-embroidered sleeves, polystavria (chasubles marked with crosses), jewelled stoles and genuals (knee coverings) – and holding open scrolls with excerpts from the Mass (fig. 33). The scenes in the bema are, unfortunately, extensively destroyed.

FIG. 32: Our Lady at Kritsa. South aisle. Apse.
Front of the apse and quarter dome. Emmanuel and St Anne.

FIG. 33: Our Lady at Kritsa. South aisle. Apse. Bema cylinder.
Officiating Bishops.

THE NAVE

In the nave, the scenes on the vault are derived from the Apocryphal Gospels and concern the conception of the Virgin and the events following her birth until the journey to Jerusalem to be taxed.

On the north part of the vault are preserved the following scenes:

JOACHIM'S TENT (ANNUNCIATION OF JOACHIM)

Joachim, a rich and devout man, always offered generously to God. However, on a great Jewish feast-day, the high priest Reuben (or Issachar) refused to accept his gifts, because God had deemed him unworthy of getting seed in Israel. Joachim was grieved by the insult and the rejection of his gifts and left his home. He withdrew into the wilderness with his shepherds and fasted in a tent with no meat and drink, praying to God to remove the curse of childlessness. After forty days, an angel of the Lord came to him and announced that his wife Anne would bear a child named Mary. According to the promise he and his wife had made, they were obliged to present her to the Temple.

In the scene of the Annunciation of Joachim, the latter is depicted sitting on the right, sad and pensive, while one of his two young shepherds, seeing the angel descending, points at Joachim in reply to the second shepherd's expression and gesture of surprise, explaining that the angel has come for their master (fig. 34).

The two shepherds are wearing western dress, Florentine hats and tight black hose tied with points. Their short tunics have long sleeves with cuffs and are gathered in by a cord on the first shepherd and a belt on the second. Both shepherds wear their belts low on their hips, according to the stylish contemporary fashion.

FIG. 34: Our Lady at Kritsa. South aisle. Vault. North side. Joachim's Tent.

Joachim, on the contrary, whose figure is shown on a larger scale, is clad in the earlier style of tunic and himation. The basic axis of the scene is diagonal, composed of the scarlet mountain, Joachim's himation of the same colour and the body of the angel. The green triangle formed by the angel's himation, the tunic of one shepherd and that of Joachim, discreetly balances the scene between the light and dark mountains in the background, while the second shepherd's off-white tunic lightens the painting and offsets the melancholy tone of Joachim's form.

THE PRAYER OF ST ANNE

During Joachim's retreat into the wilderness, St Anne, despairing at both his disappearance and her childlessness,

FIG. 35: Our Lady at Kritsa. South aisle. Vault. South side.
The Prayer of St Anne.

shut herself away in her house and refused to attend even the great religious feasts, despite the urgings of her handmaid Judith. However, she went down into the garden to walk there and sat underneath a laurel tree to pray, begging God to bless her womb as he had blessed Sarah's. Seeing a nest of sparrows in the laurel, Anne began to lament silently for her child-lessness, dramatically comparing herself unfavourably to the beasts of the earth and the fowls of heaven. At that moment an angel of the Lord descended from heaven and revealed to her that not only would she give birth, but her seed would be spoken of in the whole world.

In this scene St Anne is depicted in a walled garden with trees, birds and a fountain, elements characteristic of Paradise, standing with her hands raised in supplication to the angel. Behind her can be seen two handmaidens, the first of whom must be Judith, ecstatically watching her conversation with the angel (fig. 35).

The Greeting of Joachim and Anne

Joachim and Anne both went to the Golden Gate as the angel told them, where they met following Joachim's forty days' absence in the wilderness.

The scene depicts their meeting at the Golden Gate on Joachim's return and their respective annunciations (fig. 51). The embracing husband and wife are discreetly attended by two female household servants, depicted standing and turning slightly towards the centre, on a smaller scale that of the central figures. Although the faces of Joachim and Anne are calm, the artist shows their long mental and physical suffering by the triangular shape of Anne's face, Joachim's almost square face and the curved lines at the side of their noses, features giving them different expressions to those of their other depictions in the aisle.

At the same time, the joyful rush of their meeting is rendered by, on the one hand, the disordered drapery of Joseph's himation, whose triangular folds cover the gap between him and his wife, and, on the other, the vertical folds of Anne's maphorion over her back.

THE DWELLING OF JOACHIM

After their greeting at the Golden Gate, Joachim and Anne returned home, dined and thanked God for St Anne's Conception. The scene depicts Joachim and Anne after the annunciation of the Conception, seated on a low bench in an open area of the house. Between them is a glass wine pitcher with an upturned glass over its neck, and a young woman is waiting on them; St Anne, her eyes lifted to heaven, is thanking God for her pregnancy.

The depiction of both evokes calm, the intense emotions of the meeting having given way to a serenity of spirit (fig. 36). Anne is thanking God with her open hands, as is Joachim with his right hand raised, while his left rests on his right knee. Behind Anne, the servant girl is depicted standing and full-length with her hands extended in prayer. The faces of Joachim and Anne are fully-fleshed and rounded with a calm classical beauty, while Anne's intensely joyful face is heart-shaped, indicating the joy that filled her heart at the annunciation of her imminent pregnancy.

FIG. 36: Our Lady at Kritsa. South aisle. Vault. South side.
The Dwelling of Joachim.

THE NATIVITY OF THE VIRGIN

Nine months after the angel's appearance to Joachim and Anne, the latter bore a daughter who was named Mary in accordance with the angelic injunction.

St Anne is depicted lying on a bed immediately after the birth, in the part of the scene to the viewer's left (fig. 37). Her face has been destroyed, but it is usually rendered with a calm expression, a sign of her painless labour. Her large-scale figure constitutes the vertical axis of the scene, while a long, narrow table with a white embroidered cloth bearing fruit, vegetables and tableware forms the horizontal axis, dividing the scene into two roughly equal parts. Behind the table are three young women in rich garments and wearing strings of pearls in their hair who, together with a fourth behind St Anne, are tending the mother. In front of the table is the cradle with the swaddled baby and, beside it, yet another young woman is sitting on the floor spinning wool and minding the baby. In the background are buildings to the left and right connected by a crenellated battlement and red drapery linking the roofs. On the left, between the buildings, is a plant, probably a laurel or papyrus. Red was probably the dominant colour of the scene before its destruction, judging from St Anne's red maphorion, Mary's red cradle, the red drapery linking the

FIG. 37: Our Lady at Kritsa. South aisle. Vault. South side. Nativity of the Virgin (detail).

roofs and the red clothing of the woman behind the table who is turning towards St Anne. The green garments of the two standing women, the off-white clothing with coloured highlights of the seated woman, the white tablecloth and the off-white sides of the buildings light the scene with its brown background.

THE BLESSING OF THE VIRGIN BY THE PRIESTS

When the Virgin was a year old Joachim held a great feast and invited the priests, the Scribes, the Elders and many of his fellow-citizens. During the feast Joachim presented the child Mary to the High Priests, who blessed her, saying: *"O God of our fathers, bless this child and give her a name renowned for ever among all generations"*. Immediately afterwards, St Anne withdrew to her chamber and suckled her daughter, singing a new hymn of her own giving thanks to God who had taken away the reproach of childlessness.

The scene depicts three high priests seated behind a table with food and tableware. To the viewer's right is the Virgin being led by her mother towards the priests, two of whom are turned towards her while the third is depicted frontally, deep in prayer (fig. 38). The priests' vestments are embroidered with pearls, as are their conical head-coverings. The dominant colours of the scene are, in the figures of Anne and Mary, the red of the outer robes or himatia and the light blue-grey of the inner garments. The vestments of the high priests are of various colours. Apart from the central figure, who is depicted in a red embroidered tunic, sticharion (alb) and cloak, the others are wearing reddish sticharia with a yellow cloak for one and a green cloak for the other.

THE ADMIRATION OF THE VIRGIN

Mary remained in her parents' house until she was three years old. During this time she took only seven steps, when St Anne stood her on the ground to see if she could stand, before she was a year old. This episode is depicted in iconography as the "Heptavimatizousa" (She Who Takes Seven Steps). Immedi-

FIG. 38: Our Lady at Kritsa. South aisle. Vault. North side.
The Blessing of the Virgin by the Priests.

ately after this incident, St Anne took Mary into her arms
again, saying that she would never walk on the ground again
until she was led to the Temple of the Lord.

The scene of the Admiration, with Mary in Joachim's arms,
reminds us of Anne's decision mentioned in the Pro-
tevangelion (Pre-Gospel) Book of James, while simultane-
ously giving a picture of the love, tenderness and care with
which the divine Joachim and Anne surrounded their
daughter in the three years she was with them before her
presentation to the Temple (fig. 39).

A large section of the lower half of the scene has been destroyed. The infant Mary is depicted in her seated father's arms, wearing a short white dress embroidered with flowers. Next to them is Anne, probably also seated, holding Mary's

FIG. 39: Our Lady at Kritsa. South aisle. Vault. South side.
The Admiration of the Virgin.

foot in her left hand and raising her right in a gesture denoting speech. This depiction of Anne refers to the extract from James' Gospel mentioned above. Apart from the three main characters, the scene also shows a young woman in the background, probably one of the maidservants or the undefiled daughters of the Hebrews whom Anne had invited to her house to look after Mary. Joachim is clad in a blue-grey tunic and russet himation. Anne, as in the previous scenes, is wearing a red maphorion and blue-grey tunic, while the young woman is in a green kamision (undertunic). The scene unfolds before tall narrow buildings with two-sided tiled roofs bridged by red drapery.

THE PRESENTATION OF THE VIRGIN IN THE TEMPLE

When Mary became three years old, Joachim and Anne decided to fulfill their promise to God and take her to the Temple. As Mary was very young and they were afraid she might want to go home with them, Joachim decided to make her presentation a solemn and ritual occasion so that she would understand the sanctity of her dedication. He therefore called for undefiled daughters of the Hebrews to accompany his daughter to the Temple, each carrying a lit lamp. So Mary was led in a procession of virgins to the Temple, where she was received by the High Priest Zacharias.

The scene depicts Mary's entry into the Temple accompanied by seven virgins and their welcome by Zacharias. The figure of Mary has been destroyed, as has the whole lower part of the painting. The red colour that predominates stresses the dramatic character of the scene, the parting of a three-year-old child from her parents and especially her mother, who fulfils her oath by handing Mary to the High Priest. The artist uses red not only for Anne's maphorion and Zacharias' vestments, but also for the garment of one of the virgins watching events with covert agitation, as their different head movements and expressions show. Although restrained, Anne's sadness at being parted from her daughter is evident on her face, expressed by the slightly downturned line of her lips.

Sorrow of Joseph at the Virgin with Child

Mary lived in the Temple where she was fed by an angel. When she was twelve years old, the priests, afraid that she might pollute the Temple by the secret bodily desires arising at puberty, decided to have Zacharias the High Priest pray and ask divine guidance. When he did so, an angel of the Lord appeared and commanded him to assemble all the widowers of the people, each carrying a rod. God would show a sign indicating Mary's future betrothed.

Among the assembled widowers was a man from the tribe of David whose name was Joseph. Zacharias took all the rods, prayed and returned them. Joseph received the last rod, and at once a dove flew over his head. The High Priest understood and informed Joseph of the will of God. Joseph, however, refused, saying he was too old and Mary was too young, but his objections were overruled by fear of God's punishment. Thus he agreed to be betrothed to Mary and take her to his house, where her Annunciation took place when she was fourteen years old.

Joseph, returning to Nazareth after working in other towns, found Mary six months with child, which sank him into great sadness. He admonished her severely despite her protestation of innocence, and considered sending her away in secret without informing the priests of her crime, punishable by stoning under the law. That night an angel of the Lord appeared before him in a dream and told him that Mary was pregnant by the Holy Ghost and that she would bear the son of God.

The scene depicts, on the one hand, Joseph's sorrow at what he considers Mary's "sinful" pregnancy and his indecisiveness as to what to do, and on the other the Virgin's despair at his unjust accusations, and the angel's revelation of the truth to Joseph concerning Mary's divine mission (fig. 40). Joseph is clad in a deep-coloured tunic with red and black shading and an orange himation with brown shading; he is depicted worried and under pressure, almost sitting, holding his head and with his eyes open and anxious. The end of his himation is hanging in folds, seemingly due to his restlessness. Mary, in a blue tunic and red himation, seated on a throne on a higher

Fig. 40: Our Lady at Kritsa. South aisle. Vault. North side.
Sorrow of Joseph at the Virgin with Child.

level than Joseph, is unable to sleep, sunk in sorrow and despair. Her eyebrows are notched above the nose, which is longer and narrower, while the lips are pressed together. The angel, in a white himation with red shading, his calm face contrasting with the rush of his descent from heaven, puts an end to Joseph's torment with a revelatory vision. In the background behind Joseph and Mary are grey and violet buildings respectively, with three-arched windows and two-sided tiled roofs, decorated with anthemia (floral motifs).

THE WATER OF PROOF

After these events, Annas the scribe visited Joseph to ask why he had not been to the Temple after his return to Nazareth. Joseph excused himself saying he was weary from the journey,

FIG. 41: Our Lady at Kritsa. South aisle. Vault. North side.
The Water of Proof.

but Annas saw the Virgin great with child and went to inform
the High Priest the Joseph had defiled her. The High Priest
ascertained that Mary was indeed pregnant and called her and
Joseph to be judged. Both denied the charges, and the High
Priest decided to make them drink the water of the Lord to
reveal their sin. The drinking of the water, together with the
High Priest's curse, proved suspects' guilt by rotting their
limbs. The ordeal proved Joseph and Mary's innocence as
they were both untouched, and the High Priest let them return
home.

The scene depicts the moment of Mary's ordeal and is dominated by the form of the High Priest on a high, stepped marble throne, clad in a green tunic, a red pearl-embroidered mantle and the characteristic conical cap of Jewish priests (fig. 41). He is leaning forward towards Mary, holding the tilted water-jug which she is grasping by the neck with both hands, drinking the water of proof. Mary is depicted on a smaller scale, an indication of her youth – according to the Apocrypha she was fourteen – clad in a blue tunic and russet maphorion. Behind her, Joseph rests his left hand protectively on her shoulder, raising his right in supplication that their common innocence should shine forth. A praying servant, or perhaps one of Joseph's sons, is portrayed behind him anxiously watching the ordeal. In the background is a ciborium on pillars with a red canopy.

THE JOURNEY TO JERUSALEM

As the time for Mary to give birth approached, the Emperor Augustus ordered a census for taxation purposes of all the inhabitants of the empire including Israel. Joseph and his family, Mary and his two sons Simon and James, had to go to Bethlehem to be recorded. So he saddled his donkey for Mary and they all set out for Bethlehem, three miles away. Shortly before they reached the town, Mary felt the first labour pangs and asked Joseph to help her off the donkey. He refused because the area was uninhabited and there was nowhere to seek shelter. Mary, however, insisted and Joseph had to help her down and take her to a cave nearby, where she gave birth to Jesus.

The scene depicts this very conversation between Mary and Joseph, as indicated by the latter's frowning expression and gestures, Mary's gesture, James' turn of his head to look in her direction and Simon's questioning expression as he too looks at her (fig. 42). The pregnant Mary is depicted on a white donkey with red reins which she holds in her left hand, the only figure in the scene depicted almost frontally. At the sides of the painting, before and behind Mary and Joseph, who is following her on foot, are Joseph's two sons Simon and James,

FIG. 42: Our Lady at Kritsa. South aisle. Vault. North side.
The Journey to Bethlehem.

each carrying a staff on his shoulder and with their tunics lifted so as not to stain them on the journey.

THE SEALED GATE

The iconography of this scene is based on Ezekiel's prophecy concerning the Virgin: "*This gate shall be shut, and it shall not be opened, and no man shall enter in by it*", referring to her virginity, intact despite the conception and birth of Christ (fig. 43). The prophecy is illustrated by the depiction of the prophet Ezekiel, standing and full-length, turning slightly to his right, that is towards Mary, who is shown in a medallion with Jesus, who is wearing a green pearl-embroidered sticharion and a red mantle similarly decorated. Professor Kalokyris notes that the scene replaces that of the Nativity, which is missing from the iconographic programme of the aisle.

Fig. 43: Our Lady at Kritsa. South aisle. Vault. North side.
The Sealed Gate.

THE SCENES ON THE SIDE WALLS
AND THE WEST WALL

On the side walls of the nave, on the upper zone of decoration, are preserved three consecutive portrait busts of saints; only three are preserved on the south wall, those of St Theophano, St Theodoulos (fig. 44) and St Zoticus. The missing series of busts must have depicted the rest of the Ten Saints (Ten Martyrs of Crete): the martyrs Agathopus, Euarestus, Euporus, Gelasius, Saturninus, Eunician, Basilides and Pompeius. The portrait busts on the north wall depict the saints John the Hermit (fig. 45), Alexius the Man of God (fig.

FIGS 44-45: Our Lady at Kritsa. South aisle. North wall.
St Theodoulos and St John the Hermit.

FIGS 46-47: Our Lady at Kritsa. South aisle. North wall.
St Alexius and St Maximilian.

46), Gurias, Samonas (the depiction of the third to suffer martyrdom with the latter two, Avilus, has been destroyed), followed by the Seven Youths of Ephesus (the Seven Sleepers): Constantius (Constantine), Iamblichus, Maximilian (fig. 47), Antoninus (Antony), Exacustodian, Martinian (Martin) and John (Dionysius)

Here the artist has depicted eight youths instead of seven, depicting the seventh under both names mentioned in the sources – John and Dionysius – as if they were two different people. The martyrs are shown beardless, a sign of their youth, holding the cross in their right hand and praying with their left. They are clad in chlamydes (cloaks) clasped at the throat or shoulder, with pearl diadems on their heads. In the second, lower

FIG. 48: Our Lady at Kritsa. South aisle. North wall. St Leo.

zone of the decoration of the side walls are preserved full-length figures of saints; on the south wall there are only fragments of depictions of two hierarchs and St Theodore the Commander. The rest were destroyed by the opening of the secondary entrance. On the north wall are preserved the depictions of Deacon Romanus, in a white sticharion and

FIG. 49: Our Lady at Kritsa. South aisle. North wall.
St Irene, St Kyriake, St Barbara.

holding a thurible, ministering at the Mass to the four
hierarchs on the apse; St Leo (fig. 48), in a blue tunic and red
himation; an indiscernible saint and an archpriest – one of the
most beautiful portraits in the aisle; an archangel in imperial
garments whose portrait was cut in half by the widening of the
SE arched passageway; and the female saints Barbara,
Kyriake and Irene (fig. 49). On the west wall, on the upper
zone to the left and right of the window is the scene of St Mary
of Egypt receiving communion from St Zosimas, while under
the window is preserved the dedicatory inscription, and, to the
viewer's right, the depiction of an indiscernible military saint,
full-length and bearing a sword (fig. 50).

FIG. 50: Our Lady at Kritsa. South aisle. West wall.
St Mary of Egypt Receiving Communion from St Zosimas.
Dedicatory inscription and indistinct military sword-bearing saint.

STYLE AND DATING
OF THE WALL PAINTINGS
OF THE AISLE OF ST ANNE

The wall paintings of the aisle of St Anne are radically
different from those of the central aisle, although they do have
a point in common: the fact that they do not depict clearly-
defined interiors, as opposed to the open-air scenes, where the

countryside is presented with clarity. The architectural depth of the scenes is composed of the coloured facades of different buildings with stylised anthemia, linked by flowing red canopies.

The differences are apparent in the style – the rendition, that is, of the human form. This must be due to the dramatic historical and social changes taking place in the Byzantine Empire from the fall of Constantinople to the Crusaders at the beginning of the 13th century (1204). The break-up of the empire into various small states, resulting in the lack of a strong leadership centre, was reflected in Byzantine art, which now focussed on man and human emotions, giving new impetus to artistic freedom of expression. Thus views on the depiction of the human body and the emotionality of facial expressions changed radically.

The full-length figures are depicted relaxed, usually with their right leg forward and slightly bent, abandoning the former posture at "attention" of especially the female bodies which were also deprived of their natural curves, while the garments acquire regular folds. The similar iconographic depiction of male and female figures in the central aisle has here been abandoned. The figures acquire volume, becoming voluptuous, while the faces are more rounded and realistic. A characteristic example is that of the full-figure female saints on the south wall, depicted with substantial busts and garments caught in at the waist in a discreet contrapposto or asymmetrical arrangement, according to the classical conception. The reserved emotions of the figures of the central aisle find an outlet in those of the south aisle, through contorted facial expressions, such as those of the Virgin and Joseph in the scene of the "Sorrow of Joseph at the Virgin with Child", or the gestures and body language in "The Greeting of Joachim and Anne" (fig. 51), the impetuosity of whose embrace is rendered by the lively folds of their garments. One of the basic characteristics of the new style is the replacement of the line by chiaroscuro, giving the figures greater realism. The colours, too, become brighter and lighter and fabrics acquire metallic glints.

FIG. 51: Our Lady at Kritsa. South aisle. Vault. North side.
The Greeting of Joachim and Anne.

The new style has been named the "volume style". It originated in the region of Macedonia, with Thessalonica as its production and dissemination centre. From Thessalonica the new style was disseminated not only to the remaining free and occupied Byzantine territory, such as Crete, but throughout the Orthodox world.

The paintings of the aisle of St Anne, dated to the early 14th century, form a representative group of volume style painting as seen by Cretan popular artists. The specific iconographic programme, concerned with the human longing for children and Joachim and Anne's sorrow at their childlessness as reported in the Apocryphal Gospels, constitutes an ideal subject for the new art; it deals with an eternal issue with important human and social repercussions, while at the same time demonstrating contemporary social mores, which remain more or less unchanged today (Pl. 3, 4).

Our Lady at Kritsa. South aisle. Bema Apse. Cylinder.
St Gregory the Theologian.

PL. 3: Our Lady at Kritsa. South aisle. Volume Style.
Depiction of faces and bodies.

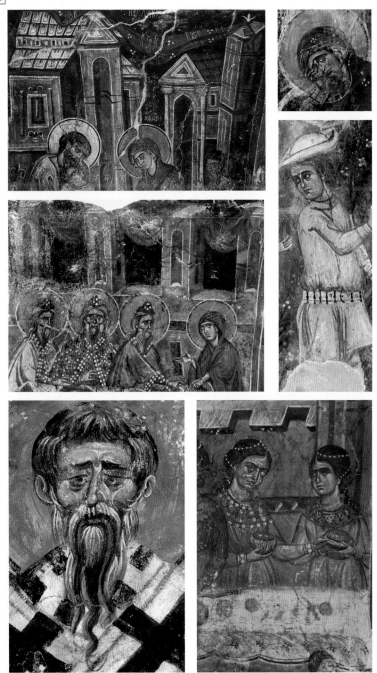

PL. 4: Our Lady at Kritsa. South aisle. Volume Style.
Buildings, expressions, fabrics.

NORTH AISLE OF ST ANTONY
BEMA APSE

On the quarter dome of the bema Christ Pantokrator, whose left side has been destroyed, is depicted in frontal bust, large-scale with an open book of the Gospels in his left hand, inscribed *"Come to me all ye that labour"*; the missing right hand would probably have been raised in a gesture of blessing.

On the cylinder of the apse is preserved the depiction of only one of the two hierarchs originally portrayed, St John Chrysostom, shown turned towards the centre of the apse,

FIG. 52: Our Lady at Kritsa. North aisle. Apse. Bema cylinder.
St John Chrysostom.

bowed before the altar which is covered with a red cloth, perhaps the antimension (consecration cloth); on the altar is a glass chalice and paten, whose contents John Chrysostom is blessing with his right hand, as the open scroll on his left hand declares: *"Make this cup..."*. The paten, chalice and scroll confirm that the scene depicts the moment of the Mass when the officiating priest blesses the bread and wine (fig. 52).

On the viewer's left is the depiction of a deacon of whom only the lower part is preserved. We can see his white sticharion, his red tunic and the ends of his stole. The representation of a deacon on the arch is found in very early decorative schemes but is extremely rare from the 12th century onwards. In Crete there are three cases, two in the district of Merambello (Our Lady at Kritsa and Our Lady at Agios Nikolaos) and the third on detached wall paintings from a church in Rethymnon Province, displayed in the Historical Museum of Heraklion.

On the front and piers of the arch of the apse, where one would normally expect depictions of the Annunciation and the deacons, is a stylised anthemion and intersecting coloured circles.

On the north wall of the bema is preserved the lower part of a depiction, probably of a second deacon, while on the north wall, apart from St John Chrysostom, are discernible traces of a second hierarch, destroyed during the widening of the north-east opening.

THE NAVE

In the nave, the depictions of the vault and west wall are exclusively dedicated to the Last Judgement, while on the long side walls are depicted isolated saints. This is a rare type of decoration.

LAST JUDGEMENT

On the south side of the vault, from east to west, are preserved the figures of John the Baptist and the Apostles, dominated by that of the Baptist, who is depicted standing and turned to the right with his head slightly inclined, clad in a tunic and himation. His dishevelled hair and frowning expression indicate the dramatic, irrevocable character of the imminent Last Judgement (fig. 53).

The Twelve Apostles are depicted frontally, in variously-coloured tunics and himatia, seated on a long backed bench

FIG. 53: Our Lady at Kritsa. North aisle. Vault. South side.
The Last Judgement. St John the Baptist and Apostles.

covered with white embroidered fabric. Each holds an open, bound Bible in his left hand with excepts concerning the Second Coming and the Last Judgement. Behind the apostles is depicted a host of angels in jewel-embroidered imperial robes.

On the soffit of the west supporting arch is depicted "*the Angel Rolling Up the Heavens*", i.e. the angel who determines the order and route of the procession of the choirs towards Christ in Judgement (fig. 54). In the scene of Paradise that follows, we see the Virgin attended by an angel on her right, and the forefathers Isaac, Abraham and Jacob with the souls of the righteous in their hands, all within the walled garden of Eden. All the figures in Paradise apart from the angel are presented seated and frontally, with the exception of the Virgin who is turning her head slightly to her right, her right hand raised in supplication, as an intermediary for the saving of the souls.

FIG. 54: Our Lady at Kritsa. North aisle. Vault. Supporting arch. South soffit. The Angel Rolling Up the Heavens.

Beneath the figures of Abraham and Jacob is the closed Gate of Paradise, guarded by the flaming sword seen at its top. Outside, St Peter, with the key in his left hand, is rushing towards the Gate, holding the Good Thief by the hand; the latter has a halo, is clad in a loincloth and is raising his right hand in supplication. In the lower left-hand corner of the scene are the four rivers of Paradise: the Phison, Gion, Tigris and Euphrates (fig. 55).

The scene depicting the Parable of the Ten Virgins covers two interstices in a vertical arrangement. Above are the five wise virgins, full-length in various poses, of whom the first two are approaching Christ who calls them to him, seated on a semi-circular arch-shaped throne with a footstool, probably symbolising heaven. Left of Christ's throne is the window of a building, while the figures of the wise virgins are superposed on tower-like buildings. In the second, rather damaged painting of the scene, are the five foolish virgins, full-length and holding extinguished lamps, moving from right to left of the scene, i.e. towards the large-scale angel waiting to announce their exclusion from Paradise. The angel's scroll is inscribed with the words "*Show your labour and receive your reward*". All ten virgins are wearing sleeved tunics with decoration at the hem, neck and sleeves, and red himatia. Their hair is decked with pearls.

FIG. 55: Our Lady at Kritsa. North aisle. Vault. South side.
Paradise.

FIG. 56: Our Lady at Kritsa. North aisle. Vault. South side.
Last Judgement. The Earth Giving Up its Dead.

FIG. 57: Our Lady at Kritsa. North aisle. West wall. Tympanum. The Angel of the Last Trump.

The decoration of the south part of the vault ends with the scene of the Earth giving up its dead (fig. 56). The Earth is depicted symbolically as a female figure wearing a diadem, surrounded by wild beasts and the four winds and seated on a beast, also crowned with a diadem. She is also encircled by a serpent drinking from a cup she holds in her right hand. Above and to the right, three of the dead in shrouds are rising from their graves at the angel's call, and among them beasts, all painted yellow, are disgorging those they have devoured.

On the west wall, a great part of whose decoration has been destroyed above and to the

FIG. 58: Our Lady at Kritsa. North aisle. West wall. Tympanum. The Weighing of Souls.

right of the window, are preserved the scenes of the Angel of the Apocalypse sounding the Last Trump over the land and sea, calling the souls to gather for the Last Judgement (fig. 57), and the Psychostasia, or Weighing of Souls. The angel, with a rushing movement expressed by the flowing folds of his green himation, sounds his trumpet in all directions for the gathering of the souls. Below is the scene of the Weighing of Souls, in which an angel bearing the scales of justice weighs the deeds of the souls and sends them to Paradise or Hell, depending on whether good outweighs evil or vice versa (fig. 58). Under the tilting scales, the form of the woman being judged is depicted small-scale and full-length, naked, with her hands crossed on her breast. In the lower zone are two scenes depicting punishments in Hell, rendered in monochrome in the western style. On the north wall is the Sea giving up its dead and the Choir of Martyrs.

THE SCENES OF THE SIDE WALLS

On the north wall is a series of saints. Those preserved are, reading from east to west, St Theodosius the Cenobiarch, much damaged, but his identity evident from the inscription on his scroll: "*if one does not reject all wordly things one cannot become a monk*"; next to him, St John Calybite is depicted full-length and frontally, in a long white and green tunic and red monk's cloak clasped at the throat. In his left hand he holds a scroll, while his right rests on his T-shaped monk's staff. The monk saint is depicted full-length and frontally, in a floor-length white and green sticharion and a russet monk's cloak.

The anonymous female saint in the following wonderful depiction is shown turning towards the bema, clad in a brown sticharion, a green monk's cloak with a clasp at the throat and a black hood.

Next to her is St Anastasia Pharmacolytria (Healer from Poison) depicted full-length and frontally in a red tunic and green sticharion (fig. 59). In her right hand is a cross and in the covered left hand a phial of antidote to poison.

St George Diasorites is portrayed mounted on a white horse and galloping left, i.e. towards the bema. Behind him on his

FIG. 59: Our Lady at Kritsa. North aisle. North wall.
St Anastasia Pharmacolytria and indistinct female saint.

horse is the maiden rescued from the dragon. The Saint is in military garb, with a bronze scale-armour breastplate and a dark blue military mantle.

The depiction of St Polychronia, very rarely included in church iconographical programmes, is mostly destroyed; she is recognisable only from the ball of earth she holds.

The series of depictions on the north wall closes with the dedicatory scene, which shows a couple with their small daughter. To the viewer's left stands the man, George Mazizanis, according to the inscription on the upper part of the painting. He is depicted large-scale and turning towards the centre of the scene, praying with his right hand; the left is not clear, but he may be resting it protectively on his daughter's back (fig. 60). He is clad in a long sleeved sticharion, a long sleeved surcoat like a kabbadion (padded garment), buttoned to below the belly and hemmed with yellow material revealed by the folds of the garment, black tied shoes with heels and black hose. On his head he is wearing a western white beguin (close-fitting cap) tied under the chin. His hair is black, reaching to the nape of the neck and escaping from under the cap in curls, while he also has a luxuriant black beard and moustache.

His wife, on the viewer's right, is portrayed almost frontally with a slight turn to the centre; she is praying with her left hand, while her right, like her husband's, is probably placed protectively on her daughter's back. She is wearing a wide, sleeved white undertunic, a white granatza (long coat with loose sleeves) with purple and a red lined mantle with tablia (embroidered panels), while her head is covered by a white kerchief. The granatza, purple and tablia indicate that the wife of George Mazizanis was of noble birth.

On the south was are depicted, from east to west, St Simon the Stylite and St Makarius, their figures almost totally destroyed; a saint, probably St Antony, in a monk's cloak and hood (fig. 61); and St Eugenius, shown frontally, with brown beard and hair, in a green sleeved sticharion and a white mantle trimmed with jewels and pearls, crowned with a wreath and holding a martyr's cross in his left hand while praying with his right, palm in front of his chest.

Fig. 60: Our Lady at Kritsa. North aisle. North wall.
The donors of the north aisle.
George Mazizanis, his wife and daughter.

St Mardarius is next, also in frontal pose, with the cross of martyrdom in his right hand and his left held in prayer before his chest. He is clad in a brown sticharion trimmed with precious stones and a blue-grey pearl-embroidered mantle.

St Orestes, in the same iconographic depiction as the rest, is wearing a long, sleeved white sticharion and a floor-length green mantle secured at the throat with a clasp. Both sticharion and mantle have pearl-embroidered hems. The saint is holding a cross in one hand and praying with the other.

St Anembodistus is shown in a floor-length, sleeved green sticharion with a jewelled hem and small crosses on the fabric, and a blue mantle. He is in the same pose as the rest.

St Mardarius, St Orestes and St Anembodistus, together with Ss Eustratius and Auxentius, are the Five Holy Martyrs, depicted in many 14th-century Cretan churches.

Fig. 61: Our Lady at Kritsa. North aisle. South wall. St Antony.

STYLE AND DATING OF THE WALL PAINTINGS
OF THE NORTH AISLE

The wall paintings of the north aisle of St Antony, although belonging to the same style as those of the aisle of St Anne, are a milder expression of it. The scene of the Last Judgement is dominated, with the exception of the angels, by figures in ceremonial, restrained attitudes. The unusual depiction of this scene across the whole vault, and the depiction of the donors on the south wall, indicate the probably funerary character of the aisle.

The apostles are depicted with handsome, expressive faces and serious expressions. Their attitudes, however, are relaxed, while their garments form soft wide folds giving the impression of velvet. The Land and Sea giving up their dead are depicted in the classical mode and with lively moulding of the features, as with the other figures. The immobility of the waiting apostles, angels, Virgin, and forefathers in Paradise is juxtaposed with the impetuous, almost violently twisting forms of the angels of the west wall and the south supporting arch, in charge of the ceremony of the Last Judgement.

The donors are excepted from the vigorous moulding of the figures, as is the case in almost all similar depictions. They are rendered with low moulding of the features, in contrast to the saints' portraits, perhaps implying that true life resides in heaven and not on earth.

The wall paintings of the aisle of St Antony, which belong, as we have said, to a later phase of the volume style, are dated to about the middle of the 14th century (Pl. 5).

PL. 5: Our Lady at Kritsa. North aisle. Volume Style.
Religious and lay facial depiction.

ΒΙΒΛΙΟΓΡΑΦΙΑ

Καλοκύρης Κ., Ο ναός της Παναγίας Κεράς στην Κριτσά Μεραμβέλλου, *Κρητικά Χρονικά* (1952), τ. 6.

Χατζηδάκης Μ., Τοιχογραφίες στην Κρήτη, *Κρητικά Χρονικά* (1952). τ. 6.

Μπούρας Χ., *Βυζαντινά σταυροθόλια με νευρώσεις*, Αθήνα 1965.

Παπαδάκη-Ökland, Στέλλα, Η Κερά της Κριτσάς: Παρατηρήσεις στη χρονολόγηση των τοιχογραφιών της, *Αρχαιολογικό Δελτίο*: Μελέτες, Μέρος Α΄ (1967), τ. 22.

Μουτσόπουλος Ν., *Η ανασκαφή της βασιλικής του Αγίου Αχιλλείου*, Θεσσαλονίκη 1972.

Βοκοτόπουλος Π., *Η εκκλησιαστική αρχιτεκτονική εις την δυτικήν Στερεάν Ελλάδα και την Ήπειρον· από του τέλους του 7ου μέχρι του τέλους του 10 αιώνος*, Θεσσαλονίκη, 1975.

Hadermann L. – Misguich L., *Kurbinovo; Les fresques de Saint – Georges et la peinture byzantine du XIIème siècle*, Bruxelles 1975.

Wessel Gallas – Borboudakis, *Byzantinisches Kreta*, München 1983.

Μπορμπουδάκης Μανώλης, *Βυζαντινές τοιχογραφίες στην Κριτσά*, α.χ. τουριστικός οδηγός.

Μπορμπουδάκης Εμμ., Η βυζαντινή τέχνη στην Κρήτη, *Ηράκλειο: Τέχνη, ιστορία και πολιτισμός*, Κρήτη 1990, τ. 2.

Γκιολές Ν., *Η βυζαντινή ναοδομία*, Αθήνα, 1990.

— *Ο βυζαντινός τρούλλος*, Αθήνα, 1990.

Μαλτέζου Χρύσα, Η Κρήτη στη διάρκεια της περιόδου της βενετοκρατίας,1211-1669, *Κρήτη: Ιστορία και πολιτισμός*, Κρήτη, 1990.

Τσουγκαράκης Δ., Η βυζαντινή Κρήτη, *Κρήτη: Ιστορία και πολιτισμός*, Κρήτη, 1990.

Μεντιδάκη Γ., *Τύπος και συμβολισμός στην ορθόδοξη λατρεία*, Ηράκλειο 1997.

Πανσελήνου Ν., *Βυζαντινή ζωγραφική. Η βυζαντινή κοινωνία και οι εικόνες της*, Αθήνα 2002.

PLAN KEY

CENTRAL AISLE

1. Archangel Michael **2.** Platytera (Virgin Wider than the Heavens) **3.** Archangel Gabriel **4.** St Nicholas **5.** St John Chrysostom **6.** Thyomenos (Christ the Sacrificed One) **7.** St Basil **8.** St Gregory **9.** Anastasis **10.** Deacon Stephen **11.** St Andrew **12.** St Titus **13.** Prophet Solomon **14.** Prophet David **15.** St Polycarp **16.** St Eleutherius **17.** Deacon Romanus **18.** St Kirykos **19.** St Panteleimon **20.** St Ermolaos **21.** St Julitta **21a.** Deesis (Virgin – Christ) **22.** Cherubim **23.** Entry into Jerusalem **24.** Raising of Lazarus **25.** Baptism **26.** Presentation in the Temple **27.** The Twelve Prophets **28.** St Matthew the Evangelist **29.** St Mark the Evangelist **30.** St John the Evangelist **31.** St Luke the Evangelist **32.** St Sergius **33.** St Mercurius **34.** St Nicetas **35.** St Bacchus **36.** Holy of Holies (Presentation of the Virgin) **37.** Last Supper **38.** Nativity **39.** Massacre of the Innocents **40.** Herod's Feast **41.** Betrayal **42.** Descent into Hell **43.** Paradise **44.** St Peter **45.** St Francis **46.** St George **47.** Elevation of the Cross (Constantine & Helen) **48.** Crucifixion **49.** Place of Torments **50.** Guardian Angel **51.** St Andrew – St Anne and Virgin.

SOUTH AISLE

1. St Anne – Emmanuel **2.** St Nicholas **3.** St Gregory **4.** St Athanasius **5.** St Eleutherius **6.** Joachim's Tent **7.** Dwelling of Joachim **8.** Prayer of St Anne **9.** Greeting of Joachim and Anne **10.** Blessing of the Priests **11.** Nativity of the Virgin **12.** Water of Proof **13.** Admiration of the Virgin **14.** Sorrow of Joseph at the Virgin with Child **15.** Presentation of the Virgin **16.** Journey to Bethlehem **17.** Sealed Gate **18.** St Zosimas **19.** Dedicatory inscription **20.** St Mary of Egypt **21.** St Irene **22.** St Kyriake **23.** St Barbara **24.** Archangel **25.** Indiscernible hierarch **26.** St Leo **27.** Deacon Romanus **28.** St John the Hermit **29.** St Alexius the Man of God **30.** St Gurias **31.** St Samonas **32.** St Constantine **33.** St Iamblichus **34.** St Maximilian **35.** St Antony **36.** St Exacustodian **37.** St Martin **38.** St John **39.** St Justin.

NORTH AISLE

1. Pantokrator **2.** St John Chrysostom **3.** Melismos **4.** Last Judgement **5.** Last Judgement **6.** Angel Rolling Up the Heavens **7.** Choir of Martyrs and Female Saints **8.** Paradise **9.** Sea Giving Up its Dead **10.** Land Giving Up its Dead **11.** Wise Virgins **12.** Foolish Virgins **13.** Angel of the Apocalypse **14.** Psychostasia (Weighing of Souls) **15.** Place of Torments **16.** Donors **17.** St Polychronia **18.** St George Diasorites **19.** St Anastasia **20.** Indiscernible female saint **21.** St John Calybite **22.** St Theodosius the Cenobiarch **23.** St Makarius **24.** St Antony **25.** St Eugenius **26.** St Mardarius **27.** St Orestes **28.** St Anembodistus.

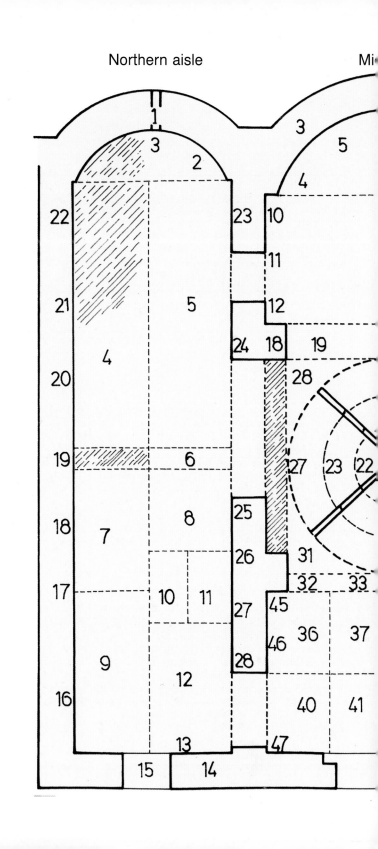

Northern aisle

Mi

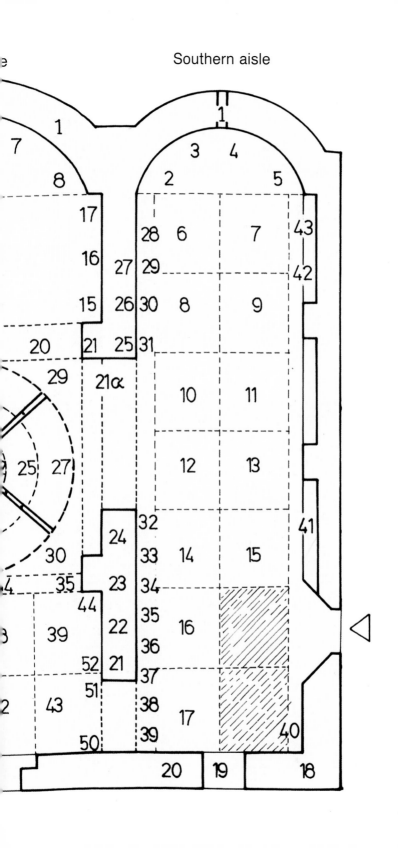